COMMANDERS

DR. STEPHANIE L. JENNINGS

MORE EXCELLENT
WAY ENTERPRISES

Publisher:
MEWE, LLC
Lithonia, GA
www.mewellc.com

First Edition
ISBN: 978-0-9988281-4-5

Library of Congress Number: 2017905892

For Worldwide Distribution
Printed in the USA

DEDICATION

*This book is dedicated to every woman who has been overwhelmed with the cares of LIFE. I want to encourage you to stop **CRYING** about the life you want and **CREATE** the life you're looking for. You're just one word away from victory!*

Acknowledgments

I acknowledge the Holy Spirit who has given me divine wisdom and supernatural intelligence to receive heaven's download and spread it throughout the earth.

I acknowledge my husband who continuously pushes me into purpose and destiny.

I acknowledge all of the "commanders," the "unsung heroes," who stand in the gap, guard the gates and watch the walls to intercept satanic activity in the earth. Please know your labor in prayer is not in vain.

I acknowledge my Publisher, Minister C. Dudley, who has kept me on track gracefully and made it possible for me to produce this manuscript.

I acknowledge my church The Harvest Tabernacle and the team of intercessors that have covered me doing the process of developing this manuscript.

I acknowledge my graphic designer, Eric Byrd, who helped me create the face to this manuscript.

Commander's Bill of Rights

- You have the right to take the earth by its edges and shake the wickedness out of it.

- You have the right to make confessions over your life.

- You have the right to bind and loose.

- You have the right to decree and declare.

- You have the right to intercede and intercept.

- You have the right to command and create.

- You have the right to watch and guard.

- You have the right to establish and employ.

- You have the right to reverse and release.

- You have the right to worship and war.

CONTENTS

But make sure that you don't get so absorbed and exhausted in taking care of all your day-by-day obligations that you lose track of the time and doze off, oblivious to God. The night is about over, dawn is about to break. Be up and awake to what God is doing! God is putting the finishing touches on the salvation work he began when we first believed. We can't afford to waste a minute, must not squander these precious daylight hours in frivolity and indulgence, in sleeping around and dissipation, in bickering and grabbing everything in sight. Get out of bed and get dressed! Don't loiter and linger, waiting until the very last minute. Dress yourselves in Christ, and be up and about!

~ **Romans 13:11-14 MSG**

STOP

Complaining

and **START**

Commanding

~ Dr. Stephanie L. Jennings

1 Commanders Arise
THE GREAT AWAKENING

Let me start by saying that prayer is more than just a friendly dialogue with God. **PRAYER IS A LIFELINE.** Prayer is agreeing with heaven concerning the pursuit of God's will in the earth. I once heard the late Myles Monroe say, "Prayer is simply getting heaven involved in earth's affairs."

Dr. Travis Jennings once said:

- "Prayer is not just informing God, but it's employing God ..."
- "Prayer is not only informing God, but it's involving God ..."
- "Prayer is not an accessory, but it's a necessity..."

As commanders, we must understand that our prayers bring heaven down to earth. And when heaven kisses earth, the essence of the kingdom will be enforced and the will of God done. Remember, God has no legal rights on earth according to Psalm 115:15-16: "*Ye are **blessed** of the LORD **which made heaven** and **earth**. The **heaven**, even the **heavens**, are the **LORD'S**: but the **earth** hath he **given** to the **children** of **men**.*" God needs human vessels in order to manifest His will in the earth. It is therefore the role of the commanders to partner with God and bring earth into alignment with heaven.

And have you ever ordered Morning, 'Get up!' told Dawn, 'Get to work!' So you could seize Earth like a blanket and shake out the wicked like cockroaches? As the sun brings everything to light, brings out all the colors and shapes, the cover of darkness is snatched from the wicked— they're caught in the very act! (Job 38:12-15 MSG)

God wanted Job to **Stop Complaining and Start Commanding.** He wanted Job to function in his full authority just as man did in the first chapter of Genesis. When God said, "*Let there be …,*" creation came into being by the words He spoke. Although Adam lost that authority through sin, the same authority has been restored to every new believer in

Christ (See Matthew 28:18-19). Just as God spoke and things came into being, so, too, can every believer speak and call forth things that do not yet exist (See Romans 4:17).

It is therefore vital that every commander understand the power of the tongue. The tongue is a small but very powerful tool for good or evil. We can bless with our tongue. We can also curse with it (See James 3:5-9). Jesus said it's not what goes into our mouth that defiles us, but what comes out of it (See Matthew 15:11). This is why satan will manipulate situations to get the commander to become agitated and fearful, so he will be tempted to make negative confessions. It is my strong conviction that if you do not like the life you are living, then **Stop Complaining and Start Commanding.** Winning begins with a word and **VICTORY** starts with the sentence: "**ALL THINGS ARE POSSIBLE**."

Commanders, let us lay hold of this promise and make a confession over our tongue according to Psalm 45:1: "*My heart is inditing a good matter: I speak of the things which I have made touching the king: my tongue is the pen of a ready writer*."

- **We DECLARE upon ourselves the tongue of the ready writer**: a learned tongue, a righteous tongue, a praying tongue, a confessing tongue, a commanding tongue, a disciplined tongue, a praising tongue, a worshiping tongue, a creative tongue, a skilled tongue, a prosperous tongue, a united tongue, a healthy tongue, a submitted tongue, a tongue that will rewrite history, a tongue that will make history, a tongue that will break every bloodline curse, a tongue that will overthrow systems, governments and strongholds; a tongue that will align heaven and earth, in Jesus' name!

- However, the enemy has many plots and plans to remove the commanders from their place of authority. 1 Peter 5:8 says it best: "*Be sober, be vigilant; because your adversary the devil, as a roaring lion, walketh about, seeking whom he may devour.*" Every commander must be on guard because the enemy is always lurking around, devising various schemes to throw him off course. Now, satan's attacks on the commander are often subtle and devious; he knows that the commander's words carry weight, so he tries to undermine the power of our words, enough to derail the waiting process that is necessary for renewing our strength (See Isaiah 40:31).

[4]

I believe that the church has been asleep for much too long now and God is awakening us and re-igniting the call to **RULE AND REIGN** on earth. It's time for the commanders to counter attack the enemy and launch a hostile takeover.

A hostile takeover is one which bypasses the board and goes straight to the shareholders of the company. In other words, God's commanders are about to confront the established systems of the world and shift things around to accommodate the will of God. Psalm 115:16 says: "*The heaven, even the heavens, are the Lord's; **but the earth hath He given to the children of men**.*"

We are the children of God and the children of men; therefore we are shareholders of this earth. We do not have to ask satan's permission to take what is rightfully ours.

SPECIAL NOTE TO COMMANDERS: The Bible says: "*From the days of John the Baptist until now the kingdom of heaven has suffered violence, and the **violent take it by force***" (Matthew 11:12 ESV). I believe that an end-time anointing is falling upon emerging commanders and we are getting ready to overthrow systems and governments, and bring down strongholds. We will refuse to take no for an answer because of the supreme power of our Commander-in-Chief and His covenant blood.

COMMANDERS, ARISE AND BUILD WITH THE WORDS THAT COME FROM YOUR MOUTH! IF GOD COULD CREATE THE WORLD IN SIX DAYS, THEN WE SHOULD BE DOING EVEN GREATER WORKS. (See John 14:12)

BEWARE OF THE ENEMIES OF PRAYER

Stay alert! Watch out for your great enemy, the devil. He prowls around like a roaring lion, looking for someone to devour.
(1 Peter 5:8, NLT)

Every commander must understand that the enemy is after his prayer life. Prayerlessness doesn't happen overnight. It's a gradual process engineered by the enemies of prayer. Their methods are subtle, so beware of these satanic agents:

- **Spirit of Religion**: man's attempt to find God through organized religion instead of a personal relationship. This spirit leads people to believe that their spiritual growth is measured by the beliefs and traditions of the religious organization they join rather than their personal relationship with God. (See Galatians 1:13-17 ASV)

- **Spirit of Heaviness**: when one is weighed down or oppressed by anxiety, sorrow, grief and sadness. It causes one to be dejected instead of rejecting satan's mind games. Praise will counter this spirit. (See Isaiah 61:3 ASV)

- **Spirit of Complacency**: when people become stagnant, stuck and lose all sense of urgency. They begin to lose their passion and purpose, and drift into a lifestyle oblivious of their spiritual condition. (See Proverbs 1:32 ESV, Proverbs 13:4 ESV, Revelation 3:15-16 ESV)

- **False Burdens**: when we have a false obligation to carry someone else's pains, problems and perplexities. This spirit will cause us to become a crutch and play God instead of allowing the individual to depend on his Burden Bearer. (See Psalm 68:19, 20 ESV, Matthew 11:29-30 ESV)

- **Carnality**: when one excessively pursues fleshly pleasures. This spirit fights against a life of pleasing God (See 1 Peter 1:14-16)

- **Fear**: causes one to surrender to phobias and become afraid of the unknown. Fear paralyzes our faith and stunts our growth (See 2 Timothy 1:7 NKJV)

- **Atmospheric spirits**: demonic activity in the atmosphere that tries to make us deviate from our destiny. This invisible force tries to hinder visible manifestations of the supernatural. (See Daniel 10:12-14 ASV, Ephesians 2:2 AMP)

COMMANDERS, we must seize the time to arise, seek God's face, resist the devil and see him flee. Romans 12:13-14 MSG declares:

But make sure that you don't get so absorbed and exhausted in taking care of all your day-

by-day obligations that you lose track of the time and doze off, oblivious to God. The night is about over, dawn is about to break. Be up and awake to what God is doing! God is putting the finishing touches on the salvation work he began when we first believed. We can't afford to waste a minute, must not squander these precious daylight hours in frivolity and indulgence, in sleeping around and dissipation, in bickering and grabbing everything in sight. Get out of bed and get dressed! Don't loiter and linger, waiting until the very last minute. Dress yourselves in Christ, and be up and about!

2 Commander's Authority
WATCHES. WITCHES. WARFARE

Nevertheless we made our prayer to our God, and because of them we set a watch against them day and night.
(Nehemiah 4:9)

Watches were shifts assigned to Israel's warriors to be on the lookout for enemies infiltrating their habitation. As commanders, we, too, must identify our watch and get on our post. While David was sitting between the inner and outer gates of the city, he saw a **watchman** going up to the roof of the gateway by the wall and a man running towards them alone, and then another. David knew they had news for him (2 Samuel 18:24-26). Here we see the role of the watchman who surveyed the land from the roof and the runner who searched the land. Their role was distinct from that of the Levites who served in the temple: "*But let no one come into the house of the Lord except the **priests** and those of the Levites who serve. They may go in, for they are holy; but **all the***

people *shall* *keep* *the* *watch* *of* *the* *LORD.*" (2 Chronicles 23:6 NKJV)

As prayer warriors and priests of the Lord, we are called to both **watch and pray.** (See Luke 21:36) Every commander must set a time to **watch and pray** according to his authority rank.

WATCHES...WITCHES...AND WARFARE

Here are the eight prayer watches according to the Bible:

FIRST WATCH (6:00 p.m. – 9:00 p.m.)
Apostolic Watch

This is the evening watch when the sun sets. This watch is for those with an apostolic pioneering anointing, who are bold in faith. It is a time of miracles, meditation, healing and deliverance. This watch breaks barriers and releases breakthroughs. (See Matthew 14:15-21, Mark 1:32-35, Luke 4:40)

SECOND WATCH (9:00 p.m. – 12:00 p.m.)
Strong Intercessors

This watch calls for strong intercessors who can take up the apostolic baton, impact the spirit realm and cancel satan's assignments. During this watch, the commander is able to jumpstart a counter attack before the enemy plots and executes our demise. (See Psalm 68:1-4, Psalm 119:62)

THIRD WATCH (12 a.m. – 3:00 a.m.)
The Witching Hour and Spiritual Warfare Time

This watch is called the witching hour because it is a transition into the darkest part of night. It is also known as the twilight between two lights. This is the time when witches and warlocks start their incantations to unleash demonic activities. During this watch we fight against the enemy of darkness. This is the time man is normally in a deep sleep, defenseless against night terrors.

The commanders who guard this watch must know how to put on their armor and exercise their authority. They must open prison doors, release divine protection, cancel all demonic activity and satanic attacks, and overrule human decrees made in the flesh. This watch also has the ability to bring about

[13]

great breakthroughs. (See Psalm 119:62, Judges 16:1-3, Job 34:20, Matthew 13:25,   Matthew 25:6, Acts 16:25)

FOURTH WATCH (3:00a.m. –6:00 a.m.)
The Commanders of the Morning and Early Risers

This watch is for the commanders of the morning and the early risers. During this watch the commander hijacks the airways from the enemy, speaks to the womb of the morning, takes the earth by its edges and shakes the wickedness out of it. (See Job 38:12-15)

This is the time to establish the course of your day and command the elements to partner with the will of God in the earthly realm. This watch is for setting the atmosphere, gaining territory, establishing true authority and releasing prosperity.

Psalm 19:6 MSG says, "*That's how God's Word vaults across the skies from sunrise to sunset, Melting ice, scorching deserts, warming hearts to faith.*" This watch requires discipline and training (See Psalm 19:2, Job 22:27-28, Matthew 14:25-33, Matthew 24:43)

FIFTH WATCH (6:00a.m. −9:00 a.m.)
The Commanders Release Strength

During this watch the Holy Spirit is preparing the commanders for service and equipping them to walk out the day in victory (See Psalm 2:7-9, Acts 2:15)

SIXTH WATCH (9:00a.m. −12:00 p.m.)
Fulfillment of God's Promises

This is the time the commander receives heavenly resources, provisions and supplies. During this watch he declares the fulfillment of God's promises and reflects on the power of God's grace and mercy (See Exodus 12:35-36, Mark 15:25)

SEVENTH WATCH (12:00p.m. − 3:00 p.m.)
Midday Attacks and Making the Most High Your Habitation

During this time, the commander must intercept satanic arrows and, at the same time, dwell in the secret place of divine protection. Midday is a time for rest as well as a time to seek the Lord. This is also the time to bind the temptations, traps and snares of the enemy. Now is the time to allow the son to shine brightly because bright vision is released at noonday (See Psalm 91:1-6, 14, Proverbs 4:18, Acts 10:9)

EIGHTH WATCH (3:00p.m. – 6:00 p.m.)
Midday Attacks and Making the Most High Your Habitation

This is the hour of dying to oneself and rejoicing in the redemptive power of Jesus Christ. During this watch Jesus died on the cross and reconciled man back to God. This is the time that the commander declares and decrees triumphant victory and resurrection power over every challenge in our lives (See Matthew 27:32-61, Philippians 1:6, Matthew 28:18-20, Ephesians 2:10, Romans 8:11)

Commanders, these eight watches will allow us to build a wall in the spirit realm that will expose the kingdom of darkness, drive out our adversary from our midst, cause us to excel in great strength, and establish God's will in the earth.

SPECIAL NOTE TO COMMANDERS: Be open to changes in your watch as you develop as a prayer warrior, grow in grace and walk in new authority.

Part I

(Ground Controllers)

3 Commander's Position

The Gates. The Guard. The Gaps

I said to them, "Do not let the gates of Jerusalem be opened until the sun is hot; and while the watchmen are still standing guard, have them shut and bar the doors. Appoint guards from the residents of Jerusalem, each at his post [on the wall], and each in front of his own house."
(Nehemiah 7:3 NASB)

Every **COMMANDER** must understand that there is an intercessor on the inside of him. It is my job to get watchmen to understand that intercession is our first responsibility no matter what our position or platform may be. Understand that intercession is not what we do, but rather who we are. We are not only people who pray but commanders who guard the gates and close the gaps between the people of God and the forces of darkness. As we link together in prayer and build a wall in the realm of the spirit, it is vital that every aspect of our wall be covered.

In the natural realm, the US Army has ground troops and the air force. This is to keep the enemy from attacking our territory both from the land and from the air. The ground troops work alongside the air force to provide protection for their nation. As commanders, we need ground soldiers to come against *satanic gravity* and air soldiers or air controllers to come against *atmospheric spirits*. As watchmen, we have been commissioned by God to intervene on behalf of others and become heaven's mouthpiece on earth.

My goal is to explain the **PURPOSE, PLEA** and **POSITION** of the ground controller. In one of Jesus' parables He said that men ought always to pray, and not to faint. One translation says we *"should always pray and never give up"* (Luke 18:1 NLT). I would like to encourage every **COMMANDER** not to ever allow the enemy to make you shut your mouth. Your words have the power to cover, command, create and conquer.

SPECIAL NOTE TO COMMANDERS: When we stop praying, we take God out of the driver's seat of our life and then we become solely responsible for any mishaps that happen along the way.

THE PURPOSE OF THE GROUND CONTROLLER

The PURPOSE of the Ground Controller is to be God's mouthpiece in the earth. Remember, according to Psalms 115:16, God has no legal authority to operate in the earthly realm. Therefore, God needs vessels to enforce His will in the earth. That's why the Bible says that in Him we live, move and have our being and greater is He that is in us than he that is in the world. (See Acts 17:28; 1 John 4:4)

The Lord needs vessels that are willing to stay between the porch and the altar to receive heaven's download and execute God's agenda in this earthly realm. Please understand that as ground controllers we have the authority to cover, command, create and conquer all satanic activity. *"On your walls, O Jerusalem, I have set watchmen; all the day and all the night they shall never be silent. You who put the Lord in remembrance, take no rest."* (Isaiah 62:6 ESV)

- **Cover** – As ground controllers we have the ability to cover all God's people in prayer. The Bible says, *"With all prayer and petition pray [with specific requests] at all times [on every occasion and in every season] in the Spirit, and with this in view, stay alert with all perseverance and petition [interceding in prayer] for all God's people. And pray for me, that words may be given to me when I open my mouth, to proclaim boldly the mystery of the good news [of salvation]."* (Ephesians 6:18-19 AMP)

- **Command** – As ground controllers we have the <u>authority</u> to command, for the Bible says, *"I assure you and most solemnly say to you, whoever says to this mountain, 'Be lifted up and thrown into the sea!' and does not doubt in his heart [in God's unlimited power], but believes that what he says is going to take place, it will be done for him [in accordance with God's will]. For this reason I am telling you, whatever things you ask for in prayer [in accordance with God's will], believe [with confident trust] that you have received them, and they will be given to you."* (Mark 11:23-24 AMP)

- **Create** – As ground controllers we have <u>power</u> to create because we are children of Abraham, *"The Scriptures says that Abraham would become the ancestor of many nations. This promise was made to Abraham because he had faith in God, who raises the dead to life and creates new things."* (Romans 4:17 CEV)

- **Conquer** – As ground controllers we can exercise our legal right to overthrow the enemy because of the finished work on the cross, *"Having canceled out the certificate of debt consisting of legal demands [which were in force] against us and which were hostile to us.*

And this certificate He has set aside and completely removed by nailing it to the cross. When He had disarmed the rulers and authorities [those supernatural forces of evil operating against us], He made a public example of them [exhibiting them as captives in His triumphal procession], having triumphed over them through the cross." (Colossians 2:14-15 AMP)

SPECIAL NOTE TO COMMANDERS - As intercessors we are prophetic snipers in the realm of the spirit and watchmen on the wall. Commanders should know their target and stay in their position.

THE PLEA (CRY) OF THE GROUND CONTROLLER

The commander must constantly offer up prayers to God for his people. We must understand that our cries move God. The Bible says, *"When the righteous cry [for help], the Lord hears and rescues them from all their distress and troubles."* (Psalms 34:17 AMP) As ground controllers we must constantly survey our land to make sure there is no illegal activity. According to Genesis 1:26-31 AMP, God said, *"Let Us (Father, Son, Holy Spirit) make man in Our image, according to Our likeness [not physical, but a spiritual personality and moral likeness]; and let them have complete authority over the fish of the sea, the birds of the air, the cattle, and over the entire earth, and*

*over everything that creeps and crawls on the earth."
So God created man in His own image, in the image
and likeness of God He created him; male and female
He created them. And God blessed them [granting
them certain authority] and said to them, Be fruitful,
multiply, and fill the earth, and subjugate it [putting it
under your power]; and rule over (dominate) the fish
of the sea, the birds of the air, and every living thing
that moves upon the earth."*

Every commander should be moving in domination
and demonstration, not in worry. *"Don't fret or worry.
Instead of worrying, pray. Let petitions and praises
shape your worries into prayers, letting God know
your concerns. Before you know it, a sense of God's
wholeness, everything coming together for good, will
come and settle you down. It's wonderful what
happens when Christ displaces worry at the center of
your life."* **(Philippians 4:6** MSG) <u>Remember your
plea shatters satan's plans and sends a signal to
heaven for angelic assistance</u>.

THE POSITION OF THE GROUND CONTROLLER

As commanders we stand on the premise of
Ephesians 2:6 ESV, that God *"has raised us up with
him, and made us to sit with him in the heavenly
places, in Christ Jesus."* This means we can go boldly
before the throne of grace. In other words, every

commander should operate at a high level of confidence, assurance and faith in God. Our position is not that of a victim, but rather a victor. One of my foundational scriptures of faith is **1 John 5:14-15 AMP**, *"This is the [remarkable degree of] confidence which we [as believers are entitled to] have before Him: that if we ask anything according to His will, [that is, consistent with His plan and purpose] He hears us. And if we know [for a fact, as indeed we do] that He hears and listens to us in whatever we ask, we [also] know [with settled and absolute knowledge] that we have [granted to us] the requests, which we have asked from Him."* Furthermore, God has given His commanders the keys to unlock and lock according to **Matthew 16:19** NIV, *"I will give you the keys of the kingdom of heaven; whatever you bind on earth will be bound in heaven, and whatever you loose on earth will be loosed in heaven."* Every commander must understand we have access to the gates, we have key to the city and we have power to guard God's people. James said, "*The prayer of a righteous person has great power as it is working*" (James 5:16 ESV).

During Nehemiah's time of building the wall he had to assign ground controllers, because of the spirit of jealousy. Let's take a look at Nehemiah, a master ground controller and magnificent strategist.

But when Sanballat, Tobiah, the Arabs, the Ammonites and the people of Ashdod heard

[25]

that the repairs to Jerusalem's walls had gone ahead and that the gaps were being closed, they were very angry. They all plotted together to come and fight against Jerusalem and stir up trouble against it. But we prayed to our God and posted a guard day and night to meet this threat. Meanwhile, the people in Judah said, "The strength of the laborers is giving out, and there is so much rubble that we cannot rebuild the wall." Also our enemies said, "Before they know it or see us, we will be right there among them and will kill them and put an end to the work." Then the Jews who lived near them came and told us ten times over, "Wherever you turn, they will attack us." Therefore I stationed some of the people behind the lowest points of the wall at the exposed places, posting them by families, with their swords, spears and bows. After I looked things over, I stood up and said to the nobles, the officials and the rest of the people, "Don't be afraid of them. Remember the Lord, who is great and awesome, and fight for your families, your sons and your daughters, your wives and your homes." <u>When our enemies heard that we were aware of their plot and that God had frustrated it, we all returned to the wall, each to our own work. From that day on, half of my men did the work, while the other half were equipped with spears, shields, bows</u>

and armor. The officers posted themselves behind all the people of Judah who were building the wall. Those who carried materials did their work with one hand and held a weapon in the other, and each of the builders wore his sword at his side as he worked. But the man who sounded the trumpet stayed with me. Then I said to the nobles, the officials and the rest of the people, "The work is extensive and spread out, and we are widely separated from each other along the wall. Wherever you hear the sound of the trumpet, join us there. Our God will fight for us!" So we continued the work with half the men holding spears, from the first light of dawn till the stars came out. At that time I also said to the people, "Have every man and his helper stay inside Jerusalem at night, so they can serve us as guards by night and as workers by day." Neither I nor my brothers nor my men nor the guards with me took off our clothes; each had his weapon, even when he went for water. (Nehemiah 4:7-23 NIV)

In this season the ground controllers will have to operate in a dual anointing. They will need to know how to defend and how to take the offensive. They will have to anticipate enemy attacks as well as go out and take territory from the enemy. Building the wall takes skills, strategy and selflessness. A

[27]

commander's job is never done because God's people are always challenged to take new heights.

COMMANDER'S SPECIAL PRAYER: Father, in the name of Jesus, we give orders to our morning and show the dawn its place; we take the earth by its edges and shake the wickedness out of it. God, let our prayers meet with You this morning. We command the morning to open its ears to our cry and we command the earth to yield the fruit and the harvest that belongs to us. We speak into our day and create new prosperity and the answer to every potential problem. We command the elements to partner with us, to take heed and obey. We stand in our rightful authority and bind all satanic activity and satanic gravity that would try to hold us down. Our hearts are dancing because this is the day that You have made. We will rejoice and be glad in it and we shout, "Send now prosperity God!" We agree with heaven and we loose the will of God in the earthly realm. We loose the full shalom of God upon every ground controller and declare, "Nothing broken and nothing missing," in Jesus' name. Amen!

Part II

(Air Traffic Controllers)

4. Commander's Position

The Gates. The Guard. The Gaps

Praise be to the God and Father of our Lord Jesus Christ, who has blessed us in the heavenly realms with every spiritual blessing in Christ. (Ephesians 1:3 NIV)

According to Ephesians 1:3, God has already blessed us in the heavenly realm. The verb **HAS BLESSED** is in the present perfect tense, indicating that something that began in the past is still continuing. This means that God has already released the blessings, and the commander must pull them down from the **heavenly realm** into the **earthly realm**. Every commander must understand that a "GAP" exists between heaven and earth.

Commanders, let's refresh our memory and reaffirm the truth about the Gaps between the realms. Do you remember Genesis 1:1: "*In the beginning God created the HEAVENS and the EARTH*"? The word **HEAVEN** in Genesis 1:1 is plural in the Hebrew source and it shows us where the first heaven was located. Now, let's jump to Genesis 1:7-8: *"And God made the firmament, and divided the waters which were under the firmament from the waters which were above the firmament: and it was so. And God called the firmament **Heaven**."*

We see that the first heaven is the earth's atmosphere. This is where the clouds form, birds fly and aircrafts travel. We call this the **SKY**. In fact, God has made three distinct heavenly places:

- ✓ **The 1st Heaven is called the SKY.** This is the earth's atmosphere, which, technically, is the *troposphere* and the *stratosphere.* (See Matthew 6:26, Revelation 19:17)

- ✓ **The 2nd Heaven is called the UNIVERSE or SPACE.** This term refers to outer space. This is where the sun, moon and stars are located. The Scriptures speak of heavenly spheres beyond the ones which are visible from the earth. This is called "the heaven of heavens." (See Deuteronomy 4:19, Matthew 24:29)

- ✓ **The 3rd Heaven, or highest heaven, is the THRONE ROOM OF GOD.** This is where God resides and it is not limited to a geographical location. (See Deuteronomy 10:14, Hebrews 8:1)

Here is where the problem in our understanding lies. God releases our blessings from His throne room in the third heaven. However, in order for us to receive the tangible manifestation of the blessing, it has to pass through the second and first heaven. Now remember that Ephesians 2:2 states that satan is "*the prince of the power of the air.*" Even though God has given the earth to the sons of man and calls us kings and priests unto Him, we still have to fight an endless battle with spiritual forces in order to see the promises of God materialize.

Do you remember the tenth chapter of Daniel? After he fasted and cried out to God for three whole weeks, Daniel's answer finally came on the twenty-first day.

> *Then he said, "Don't be frightened, Daniel, for your request has been heard in heaven and was answered the very first day you began to fast before the Lord and pray for understanding; that very day I was sent here to meet you. But for twenty-one days the mighty Evil Spirit who overrules the kingdom of Persia blocked my way. Then Michael, one of the top officers of the heavenly army, came to help me, so that I was able to break through these spirit rulers of Persia."* (Daniel 10:12-13 TLB)

SPECIAL NOTE TO COMMANDERS: Atmospheric spirits represent demonic activity in the atmosphere and second heaven that seeks to deter us from the course of our destiny. These invisible forces try to hinder the tangible blessing from manifesting. Do you now see how God releases the blessings and satan sets up barriers called **Atmospheric Spirits** to block the blessings from getting down to the earthly realm?

One day during prayer, I heard the Lord say, "You need an **AIR TRAFFIC CONTROLLER**."

In the **natural realm** Air Traffic Controllers are known as ATCs. They direct aircraft on the ground and through controlled airspace. They also provide advisory services to aircraft in non-controlled airspace. These ATCs are people trained to maintain the safe, orderly and expeditious flow of air traffic in the global air traffic control system.

The position of air traffic controller is one that requires **highly specialized knowledge, skills** and **abilities**.

In the **spiritual realm** Air Traffic Controllers are Intercessors trained to **maintain the safe**, **orderly** and **expeditious flow of the release from heaven to earth**. These are sharp shooters in the realm of the Spirit who will take out all atmospheric spirits that try to hinder God's plan from manifesting on earth.

- **Joshua was an Air Traffic Controller**
The Lord was helping the Israelites defeat the Amorites in battle. So about noon, Joshua prayed to the Lord loud enough for the Israelites to hear: "O Lord, make the sun stop in the sky over Gibeon, and the moon stand still over Aijalon Valley."'

This poem can be also found in The Book of Jashar. So the sun and the moon stopped and stood still until Israel defeated its enemies. The sun stood still and did not go down for about a whole day. Never before and never since has the Lord done anything like that for someone who prayed. The Lord was really fighting on behalf of Israel. (Joshua 10:12-14 CEV)

- **David was an Air Traffic Controller**
David answered Goliath: You've come out to fight me with a sword and a spear and a dagger. But I've come out to fight you in the name of the Lord All-Powerful. He is the God of Israel's army, and you have insulted him too!

Today the Lord will help me defeat you. I'll knock you down and cut off your head, and I'll feed the bodies of the other Philistine soldiers to the birds and wild animals. Then the whole world will know that Israel has a real God. Everybody here will see that the Lord doesn't need swords or spears to save his people. The Lord always wins his battles, and he will help us defeat you.

When Goliath started forward, David ran toward him. He put a rock in his sling and swung the sling around by its straps. When he let go of one strap, the rock flew out and hit Goliath on the forehead. It cracked his skull, and he fell face down on the ground. David defeated Goliath with a sling and a rock. He killed him without even using a sword. (1 Samuel 17:45-50 CEV)

- **Elijah was an Air Traffic Controller**
Elijah told Ahab, "Get something to eat and drink. I hear a heavy rain coming."

Ahab left, but Elijah climbed back to the top of Mount Carmel. Then he stooped down with his face almost to the ground and said to his servant, "Look toward the sea."

The servant left. And when he came back, he said, "I looked, but I didn't see anything." Elijah told him to look seven more times.

After the seventh time the servant replied, "I see a small cloud coming this way. But it's no bigger than a fist."

Elijah told him, "Tell Ahab to get his chariot ready and start home now. Otherwise, the rain will stop him."

A few minutes later, it got very cloudy and windy, and rain started pouring down. So Elijah wrapped his coat around himself, and the Lord gave him strength to run all the way to Jezreel. Ahab followed him. (1 Kings 18:41-46 CEV)

- **Jesus was an Air Traffic Controller**
That evening, Jesus said to his disciples, "Let's cross to the east side." So they left the crowd, and his disciples started across the lake with him in the boat. Some other boats followed along. Suddenly a windstorm struck the lake. Waves started splashing into the boat, and it was about to sink.

Jesus was in the back of the boat with his head on a pillow, and he was asleep. His disciples woke him and said, "Teacher, don't you care that we're about to drown?"

Jesus got up and ordered the wind and the waves to be quiet. The wind stopped, and everything was calm.

Jesus asked his disciples, "Why were you afraid? Don't you have any faith?"

Now they were more afraid than ever and said to each other, "Who is this? Even the wind and the waves obey him!" (Mark 4:35-41 CEV)

These air traffic controllers used their vocal cords to break barriers and release breakthroughs for God's people. Their perseverance led to miracles.

It is my belief that God is raising up a company of air traffic controllers (intercessors) who refuse to surrender to the enemy and any kind of opposition. These intercessors have embraced their processing and are walking in their destiny. They have taken ownership of their times of chastening and understand that their pain has given them access to an even greater anointing.

Commanders must also understand that what is done in private will eventually go public. This is why the air traffic controllers as priests stay between the porch and the altar of public and private life.

As commanders we must firmly believe that we have the upper hand over every atmospheric spirit. No weapon formed against us will prosper.

We have been equipped with the right tools and strategies to win in every challenge.

COMMANDERS possess **voice activation power**, **voice deactivation power** and **voice command power** to enforce God's rules.

We activate these powers through **binding** and **loosing**, **decreeing** and **declaring.**

We realize that wherever there is extreme victory, there has been extreme warfare. Commanders, are you ready?

BINDING AND LOOSING

Binding and loosing is a way of taking control over atmospheric spirits -- satanic activities and territorial spirits. When the commanders bind and loose, they draw up a contract in the realm of the spirit and close the "gap" between heaven and earth.
They establish real authority. Commanders always remember that God gave the earth to the sons of man, but satan is the prince of the power of the air, according to Ephesians 2:2.

Moreover, satan has some authority, but not absolute authority. But we, the redeemed of the Lord, can claim back the authority we have already been given in Christ.

> *And Jesus came and spake unto them, saying, **ALL** power is given unto me in heaven and in earth. Go ye therefore, and teach all nations, baptizing them in the name of the Father, and of the Son, and of the Holy Ghost …* (Matthew 28:18-19)

> *I will give you the keys (authority) of the kingdom of heaven; and whatever you bind [forbid, declare to be improper and unlawful] on earth will have [already] been bound in heaven, and whatever you loose [permit, declare lawful] on earth will have [already] been loosed in heaven.* (Matthew 16:19, AMP)

DECREEING

A decree is defined as a rule of law issued by the head of state. In biblical times, the king had the authority to make decrees which were enshrined in a written document. Since they were considered law, the decrees were binding and enforceable according to the king's wishes. If one failed to comply, he would be punished.

According to Revelation 1:6, all believers are kings and priests unto God. As kings and priests, we, too, have the authority to make decrees:

> *You will also decide and decree a thing,*
> *and it will be established for you; and*
> *the light [of God's favor] will shine upon*
> *your ways.* (Job 22:28, AMP)

As commanders we have the authority to speak to the womb of the morning and command it to give birth to the will of God concerning our lives. We have the tongue of the learned and we can go in and out of spiritual atmospheres and take possession of earthly blessings.

DECLARING

Declaring is speaking into the atmosphere and making known what Christ has already accomplished on the cross. In other words, we make an announcement reaffirming the finished work of Christ.

> *Declaring the end and the result from the*
> *beginning, and from ancient times the*
> *things which have not [yet] been done,*
> *Saying, 'My purpose will be established,*
> *And I will do all that pleases Me and*
> *fulfills My purpose.'* (Isaiah 46:10 AMP)

[41]

This is the confidence that every commander must walk in. According to Romans 8:28, our declarations are working out for good. God's plan will prevail over every atmospheric spirit and His purposes will manifest in the earth.

5 Commander's Posture

Acknowledgment. Recognition. Expression

For it is written, "As I live," says the Lord, "every knee shall bow to me, and every tongue shall confess to God." So then each of us will give an account of himself to God.
(Romans 14:11-12 ESV)

COMMANDER'S POSTURE

A commander's posture during prayer is determined by the prayer assignment given. The commander should always be flexible and open to the voice of God when it comes to his posture during prayer. Your prayer watch may determine your posture. Your posture may also depict your acknowledgment, recognition and expression of your heart towards God.

BOWING BEFORE THE KING

Bowing before the King of kings shows the honor and allegiance we give to God. As commanders we must have the heart of a worshiper, and when we bow we acknowledge God as the Supreme Authority. Be mindful that bowing our head sends a message to our mind that we are addressing someone of power and authority. Before such a great power we should take on a humble posture.

- *All the sons of Israel, seeing the fire come down and the glory of the LORD upon the house, bowed down on the pavement with their faces to the ground, and they worshiped and gave praise to the LORD, saying, "Truly He is good, truly His loving kindness is everlasting."* (2 Chronicles 7:3 NASB)

- *Now at the completion of the burnt offerings, the king and all who were present with him bowed down and worshiped. (*2 Chronicles 29:29 NASB)

- *I have sworn by Myself, The word has gone forth from My mouth in righteousness And will not turn back, That to Me every knee will bow, every tongue will swear allegiance.* (Isaiah 45:23 NASB)

- *And Moses quickly bowed his head toward the earth and worshiped.* (Exodus 34:8 ESV)

KNEELING BEFORE THE KING

Kneeling before the King of kings acknowledges His rulership over us. As commanders we acknowledge that Jesus is not only our Lord but also our King.

Commanders should always remember that we submit and answer to a higher authority. The greatest leaders recognize their King.

- *Come, let us worship and bow down, Let us kneel before the LORD our Maker.* (Psalm 95:6)

- *Solomon had made a bronze platform five cubits long, five cubits wide, and three cubits high, and had set it in the court, and he stood on it. Then he knelt on his knees in the presence of all the assembly of Israel, and spread out his hands toward heaven, and said, "O Lord, God of Israel, there is no God like you, in heaven or on earth, keeping covenant and showing steadfast love to your servants who walk before you with all their heart ..."* (2 Chronicles 6:13-14 ESV)

- *Therefore God has highly exalted him and bestowed on him the name that is above every name, so that at the name of Jesus every knee should bow, in heaven and on earth and under the earth, and every tongue confess that Jesus Christ is Lord, to the glory of God the Father.* (Philippians 2:9-11 ESV)

- *When Daniel knew that the document had been signed, he went to his house where he had windows in his upper chamber open toward Jerusalem. He got down on his knees three times a day and prayed and gave thanks before his God, as he had done previously.* (Daniel 6:10 ESV)

LYING PROSTRATE BEFORE OUR LORD

Sometimes bowing and kneeling may not adequately express the attitude of our heart or the intent of our worship. However, lying prostrate is an open demonstration of an inward cry.

When a commander lies prostrate, it causes his flesh to submit to the Lordship of Jesus Christ. It sends a signal to Him that we are throwing ourselves at His mercy.

- *So I lay prostrate before the LORD for these forty days and forty nights, because the LORD had said he would destroy you.* (Deuteronomy 9:25 ESV)

- *And Ezra blessed the Lord, the great God, and all the people answered, "Amen, Amen," lifting up their hands. And they bowed their heads and worshiped the Lord with their faces to the ground.* (Nehemiah 8:6)

- *And going a little farther he fell on his face and prayed, saying, "My Father, if it be possible, let this cup pass from me; nevertheless, not as I will, but as you will."* (Matthew 26:39 ESV)

LIFTING HANDS BEFORE OUR GOD

When the commander lifts his hands before God it shows his vulnerability and openness. Uplifted hands are an expression of the commander's heart and a sign of his total surrender to God.

- *So I will bless you as long as I live; in your name I will lift up my hands.* (Psalm 63:4 ESV)

- *I desire then that in every place the men should pray, lifting holy hands without anger or quarreling.* (1 Timothy 2:8 ESV)

- *Lift up your hands to the holy place and bless the Lord!* (Psalm 134:2 ESV)

LIFTED EYES BEFORE OUR SAVIOR

Lifted eyes before our Savior shows a steadfast faith and focus. Commanders, I know it is very tempting to close your eyes during prayer to eliminate all distractions, but Jesus told his disciples, "Watch as well as pray." Our eyes should stay fixed on our Savoir to show our dependency on His strength.

- *I lift up my eyes to the hills. From where does my help come? My help comes from the Lord, who made heaven and earth.* (Psalms 121:1-2 ESV)

- *Jesus spoke these things; and lifting up His eyes to heaven, He said, "Father, the hour has come; glorify Your Son, that the Son may glorify You." (John 17:1 NASB)*

- *And taking the five loaves and the two fish, he looked up to heaven and said a blessing over them. Then he broke the loaves and gave them to the disciples to set before the crowd.* (Luke 9:16 ESV)

SILENCE IN THE PRESENCE OF GOD

As commanders sometimes we must learn to be silent in the presence of God. We must understand that it's not always what we say, but also what we hear. Being silent in the presence of God takes a disciplined ear, because one must be trained to hear the voice of God.

I'm reminded of the time God spoke to Elijah in a still small voice. This type of posture goes beyond physical boundaries into the spiritual realm. It speaks of the commander's maturity in his walk with Christ. In the natural it is easy to talk but harder to listen. Every commander should practice this posture of stillness.

- *Be still, and know that I am God. I will be exalted among the nations, I will be exalted in the earth!* (Psalms 46:10 ESV)

- *Hannah was speaking in her heart; only her lips moved, and her voice was not heard. Therefore Eli took her to be a drunken woman.* (1 Samuel 1:13 ESV)

STANDING IN THE PRESENCE OF A KING

Standing in the presence of a king is an honor and privilege. This posture has been used during public worship and corporate prayer since biblical times. To stand signifies great respect and reverence. As commanders, this method is important because it shows acknowledgment and recognition of the

Supreme Authority present. Whenever God's people stood together it brought down a greater glory.

- *And Jehoshaphat stood in the assembly of Judah and Jerusalem, in the house of the Lord, before the new court, and said, "O Lord, God of our fathers, are you not God in heaven? You rule over all the kingdoms of the nations. In your hand are power and might, so that none is able to withstand you."* (2 Chronicles 20:5-6 ESV)

- *Then the king turned around and blessed all the assembly of Israel, while all the assembly of Israel stood.* (2 Chronicles 6:3 ESV)

- *Therefore keep the words of this covenant and do them that you may prosper in all that you do. You are standing today, all of you, before the Lord your God: the heads of your tribes, your elders, and your officers, all the men of Israel, your little ones, your wives, and the sojourner who is in your camp, from the one who chops your wood to the one who draws your water, so that you may enter into the sworn covenant of the Lord your God, which the Lord your God is making with you today.* (Deuteronomy 29:9-12 ESV)

I WOULD RATHER
TEACH
ONE MAN TO
PRAY
THAN TEN MEN TO
PREACH

~ Charles Spurgeon

6 Commander's Prayer Tips

Beginner.

Intermediate.

Advanced.

Commander's Prayer Tips for Beginners
~TIPS FOR ENHANCING YOUR PRAYER LIFE~

First of all, I would like to commend you for accepting the responsibility of becoming a commander. Building a prayer life takes time and discipline. Below are some quick tips to assist you in becoming a strong intercessor. Remember not to judge your prayer life based on others around you, but keep to your own pace and watch God elevate you during the process. Try to pray at least 15 to 20 minutes for the first 30 days.

- ✓ **Pray at the beginning of your day.**

- ✓ **Plan to meet God every morning at the same time.**

- ✓ **Set a specific place for prayer.**

- ✓ **Set an atmosphere for prayer by playing your favorite worship music.**

- ✓ **Write down at least 10 Bible verses to recite during prayer.**

- ✓ **Always bring your Bible, notepad and pen to prayer.**

(Remember you're building a prayer life; therefore I strongly encourage you to use a physical Bible instead of a digital one to eliminate distractions and temptations.)

✓ **Start studying about the full armor of God and why it is necessary to put it on daily.**
(This may be found in Ephesians 6:10-17.)

✓ **Write down your prayer list or prayer targets.**
(This will help you stay focused during prayer and keep your mind from wandering.)

✓ **Start off your prayer with <u>adoration</u>, <u>praise</u>, <u>thanksgiving</u> and <u>petition</u>.**

- **Adoration:** This is when you express your love towards God.

- **Praise:** This is when you extol God for His mighty acts.

- **Thanksgiving:** This is when you express your thankfulness for God's grace and mercy.

- **Petition:** This is when you make a specific prayer request to God.

Commander's Prayer Tips for Intermediate
~TIPS FOR ENHANCING YOUR PRAYER LIFE~

Are you ready to add on more features to your prayer life? By now prayer is not what you do, but who you are. During this phase we are going to teach you more prayer strategies for becoming an effective intercessor.

- ✓ **Begin your prayer with the spirit of worship.**
  (This means you don't necessarily need music because worship is exuding from you.)

- ✓ **I still suggest you meet God at the same time every day.**
  (The time of the day in which you pray might change.)

- ✓ **Make sure you put on the whole armor of God daily.**
  (During this phase your prayer time may change. See chapter 8.)

- ✓ **We are now learning how to pray on specific topics.**
  (Write down 15 to 20 Bible verses on a specific subject and recite them during prayer.)

✓ **Join the intercessory prayer team at your local church assembly. This will teach you how to pray with other commanders.**
(This will also keep you connected and cut any fleshly desires that may try to flare up as you enhance your prayer life.)

✓ **Start creating a prayer vocabulary notebook.**
(You must learn specific terms used in prayer and their meanings. Make sure you don't use words above your spiritual authority. Only flow from your grace point.)

✓ **Learn what is fighting against you during your time of prayer.**
(See chapter 8 for more details.)

✓ **You should know satan's names and their functions.**

✓ **By now you should know how to pray in your supernatural language and pray the word of God.**
(This should be a part of your daily regimen.)

Commanders' Prayer Tips for Advanced
~TIPS FOR ADVANCING YOUR PRAYER LIFE~

If you have made it thus far, you have been diligent, consistent and faithful enough to becoming an advanced commander. You understand the importance of prayer and its impact on advancing the kingdom of God. By now you also should be a skilled intercessor.

- ✓ **You should know your prayer WATCH.**

- ✓ **You should know what <u>principality rules</u> in your REGION.**

- ✓ **You should be FLUENT in <u>prayer terminology</u> and skilled in the usage of the words.**

- ✓ **You should have <u>specific prayer</u> ASSIGNMENTS.**

- ✓ **You should learn the names of demonic spirits and their meaning.**
  (This should be added to your prayer vocabulary notebook.)

- ✓ **You should be able to discern different spiritual atmospheres.**

[58]

✓ **You should be able to shift spiritual atmospheres.**

✓ **You should know how to pray without ceasing.**
(This simply means you should always be aware of God's presence and sensitive to His voice. Prayer has now become a way of LIFE.)

✓ **You should be praying and fasting.**

✓ **You should know how to let the high praises of God be in your mouth and two-edged sword in your hand.**
(This requires great skill and discipline.)

✓ **You understand the importance of prayer teams and the power of agreement.**

7 Commander's 21-Day Prayer Guide
Prayers that Break Barriers and Bring Breakthroughs

DAY **1**

Today we decree and declare that the commanders will arise in power and might. We take the earth by its edges and shake the wickedness out of it. Lord, rain upon Zion and let the heavens pour out Your blessings exceedingly abundantly. We decree and declare restoration has come from anything stolen by the enemy from our lives. We rebuke the waves of misfortune that would try to overwhelm us, and we declare the flood will not drown us. Lord, let this year be filled with uncommon favor and unusual blessings. We rebuke every atmospheric spirit and satanic gravity that will try to hinder and hold our promises.

Today, we leap into alignment with the will of God and declare that the nations will receive deliverance on Mount Zion, and we will reclaim our possessions. We decree and declare that every ministry will be vindicated in front of our enemies and releases will flow. We command every mountain that has been blocking our healing, deliverance, breakthrough, possibilities, opportunities, potential, prosperity, favor and increase to be removed. We take the mantle of Abraham and step out in faith and go from stuck to unstoppable. We command every light bringer to come forth and be an expression of God's glory in the earth realm. We decree and declare that we are mountain movers, momentum shifters and mantle carriers. We walk in an apostolic and prophetic mandate. We declare that the next thirty days will be full of divine connections, divine directions, divine steps, holy boldness and new authority. We decree and declare no more dead-ends. We decree and declare freedom and the full Shalom of God upon us, nothing broken and nothing missing. Father, we thank You for connecting us with our Boaz and our Abraham, who will help fund every righteous cause. We decree and declare that Your commanders will walk in green pastures, healthy pastures and whole pastures. We decree and declare that the commanders are arising and taking territory in Jesus' name!

DAY 2

Father, let the rest of this year be full of FAVOR, FORTUNE AND FIGHT. Today we stand on the promise of Matthew 7:11 ESV, "If you then, who are evil, know how to give good gifts to your children, how much more will your Father who is in heaven give good things to those who ask him!" This morning we take the earth by its edges and shake the wickedness out of it. We shake out spirits of sabotage, self-sabotage, misfortune, poverty, lack, generational curses, generational cycles, generational circles, generational stagnation and generational mindsets. Lord, You've established Psalm 24:1 in the heavens and on the earth, so we decree: "The earth is the LORD's 'and the fullness thereof they that dwell therein." We decree and declare open doors of opportunity for Your people. We decree and declare a week of exceeding abundance, a week of more than we can ask or think. We decree and declare NEW DOORS, NEW FORTUNES, NEW FIGHT, NEW STRENGTH, NEW VICTORIES AND NEW MOMENTUM. We decree and declare the manifestation of our promises, in JESUS' name!

DAY 3

Father, let the full Shalom of God be upon us, nothing broken and nothing missing. Today we take the earth by its edges and shake the wickedness out of it. We shake out mind racing, harassing thoughts, anxieties, nervous expectations, false burdens and emotional contracts with wolves in sheep's clothing.

We decree and declare that we will trust in Your word, and rest in Your promises, plans and purposes for our lives. We decree and declare that today is the day that the Lord has made and we will rejoice and be glad in it! We stand on the promises of

- Psalm 62:1-2 NIV: *My soul finds rest in God alone; my salvation comes from him. He alone is my rock and my salvation; he is my fortress, I will never be shaken.*

- Leviticus 25:4 ESV: *But in the seventh year there shall be a Sabbath of solemn rest for the land, a Sabbath to the Lord. You shall not sow your field or prune your vineyard.*

- Psalm 73:26 ESV: *My flesh and my heart may fail, but God is the strength of my heart and my portion forever.*

- Psalm 61:1-4 NIV: *Hear my cry, O God; listen to my prayer. From the ends of the earth I call to you, I call as my heart grows faint; lead me to the rock that is higher than I. For you have been my refuge, a strong tower against the foe. I long to dwell in your tent forever and take refuge in the shelter of your wings.*

- Isaiah 40:28-31 NIV: *Do you not know? Have you not heard? The Lord is the everlasting God, the Creator of the ends of the earth. He will not grow tired or weary, and his understanding no one can fathom. He gives strength to the weary and increases the power of the weak. Even youths grow tired and weary, and young men stumble and fall; but those who hope in the Lord will renew their strength. They will soar on wings like eagles; they will run and not grow weary, they will walk and not be faint.*

- Hebrews 4:9-11 ESV: *So then, there remains a Sabbath rest for the people of God, for whoever has entered God's rest has also rested from his works as God did from his. Let us therefore strive to enter that rest, so that no one may fall by the same sort of disobedience.*

- Hebrews 4:16 ESV: *For we do not have a high priest who is unable to sympathize with our weaknesses, but we have one who in every respect has been tested as we are, yet without sin. Let us therefore approach the throne of grace with boldness, so that we may receive mercy and find grace to help in time of need.*

- Matthew 11:28 NIV: *Come to me, all who are weary and burdened, and I will give you rest. Take my yoke upon you and learn from me, for I am gentle and humble in heart, and you will find rest for your souls.*

We decree and declare that today will be a day of total rest and restoration, in Jesus' name!

DAY **4**

Father, we rise this morning to say, Thank You! Thank You for commanding Your love towards us! Today we stand in agreement and pray for our city. We thank

You for a gentleness in our city, love in our city, joy in our city, faith in our city, increase in our city, stability in our city, strength in our city, wise counsel in our city, and we declare safety in our city. We cover our governors, mayors, city counselors and city officials today. We decree and declare that they will walk in divine wisdom to lead our cities.

We pray for the release of noble men in our city, the release of men of character, men of valor, apostles, prophets and pastors in our city.

We bind hatred, racism and discrimination in our city. We bind the strongman of lust and perversion in our city. We bind all spirits that come to torment us in our city. Lord, raise up those with a Shamar anointing to guard and protect our cities.

We decree and declare that our city will be a place that glorifies God. We decree and declare prosperity. We decree and declare purity and prayer coming to our cities. We declare the rain of Holy Ghost revival and salvation upon our city.

We decree and declare a turnaround in our city, in Jesus' name.

DAY 5 ———————————————

Father, we thank You for Your love lifting us from a place of despair, discouragement and devastation. Today we stand on Psalm 30:1-5 and shout, Thank You for keeping us alive and not letting us sink into the deep. Today we sing praises to our Lord because praise belongs to You. We give thanks to Your holy name. For Your anger is but for a moment and Your favor is for a lifetime. Weeping may endure for the night, but joy comes in the morning. As for us, we shout, "Send now prosperity!"

We employ the host of heaven to war against the hosts of darkness and command every atmospheric spirit, demonic movement and satanic activity to cease from operating in our lives. We decree and declare that praise is on our lips and will become the meditation of our hearts because our hallelujahs belong to You! We decree and declare a lifting of our finances, fortunes and future. God, lift every heavy load hung over our heads and problems that weigh us down, and heal the broken hearted, in Jesus' name!

DAY 6

Father, we thank You for POWER over all diseases and ailments. We apply the powerful, redeeming blood of Jesus upon ourselves from the crown of our head to the soles of our feet. We apply the blood on our muscular systems, skeletal system and respiratory system. We bind all allergies and sinus infections. We bind all skin cancer, throat cancer, bladder cancer, breast cancer, lung cancer, prostate cancer, pancreatic cancer, colon and rectal cancer, leukemia, kidney cancer, thyroid cancer, skin rashes, allergies, eating disorders, ear ailments and disabilities, and we decree and declare healing, in Jesus' name! We come against forgetfulness and chronic pain. We come against the spirits that interfere with Your divine precision in our liver, hearts, lungs, bladder and intestines. We bind all forms of personality disorders. We command high cholesterol, low cholesterol and insulin levels to be normal. We bind all skin ailments: eczema and rash breakouts, and alopecia. We speak to ear problems, eye problems; near sightedness, farsightedness; astigmatism, and we command our body to function in the perfection that God created it to function.

[69]

Father, You are the Miracle Worker and You said that whatsoever we bind on earth shall be bound in heaven and whatsoever we loose on earth shall be loosed in heaven (See Matthew 16:19). So now, we take authority over the strongman of disease and sickness. We plead the blood over every tumor, all forms of cancer, HIV and AIDS, and we command them to dissolve and dry up by the roots, in Jesus' name (See Matthew 20:21-22). For, by Your stripes we are healed (See Isaiah 53:5). We decree and declare that divine healing and divine restoration for Your people will take place now!

We command the brain to function properly and all migraines, depression, drug abuse, dysfunctions and writer's block to go now. We make a demand on Your word and we receive divine intelligence and supernatural wisdom. We come against the chemicals that are released in the brain that cause addictive behaviors and we command righteous thoughts and holy behaviors.

This is the day of a NEW ERA - New health, New wealth, New flow and a New move of God! Father, because we walk in Your healing, we thank You for promotion. Use us to demonstrate Your glory. Today will be a day of intellectual release! Holy Spirit, we ask of You to go before us and prepare the way. Every ditch that has been dug by the enemy is being exposed now. The Lord has ordered our steps. There is a dam-breaking anointing being released now and everything that was held back is beginning to flow again.

Our creativity is getting ready to flow. We have the power to make the RIGHT MOVES, RIGHT DECISIONS and RIGHT STEPS, in the name of Jesus. Death is rebuked now! We declare that the doctors will be amazed at the recovery of the saints of God! Our bodies are operating at optimum level and they are able to carry the weight of our assignment. We will accomplish and fulfill our destiny. Today will be an exceptional day, in Jesus' name!

DAY 7

Father, we honor You and thank You for Your grace and mercy. We thank You for a new season and new garments. We thank You for this opportunity to show forth Your glory in the earth. Today, we put on the Garment of righteousness, sanctification, intelligence, revelation, power, counsel, might, strength and wisdom, in Jesus' name. Today, we receive Your love, kindness and goodness. We prophesy over our lives that every spoken promise and every blessing that has been held up will manifest in our lives, now. We speak as the oracles of God and we command satan to loose your hold, now!

We prophesy that this is the season of an open heaven and we will receive angelic assistance. We command our angels to go to work and bring in our harvest. God, raise up people to use their power, influence and ability to help us.

We decree and declare favor with all men from the north, south, east and west. We anoint our hands to bring wealth into our lives. We decree and declare we will touch NEW THINGS. We bind every delaying tactic of the enemy. We loose provision, protection and prosperity over our lives. We will not walk in stress or anxiety, in Jesus' name. This is the season of great peace, and we walk in the complete Shalom of God, nothing broken and nothing missing.

We decree that everything You have promised will be made manifest, and we will see Your goodness! We decree and declare an acceleration of our manifestation. We decree and declare multiple testimonies all at once. We decree and declare that today is a NEW SEASON, and BLESSINGS are getting ready to FALL, in Jesus' name!

DAY 8

Good morning, Holy Spirit! We arise this morning and take the earth by its edges and shake the wickedness out of it. We command the earth and the elements to partner with the will of God concerning our lives. We decree and declare that You, Father, are REBOOTING, REBUILDING AND REFRESHING Your people. Father, we thank You for an AMAZING ... ASTOUNDING ... ACHIEVING week. We decree and declare this will be the year of accomplishments, and every week we look to You to do something NEW!

We decree and declare this week that we will be more, do more, achieve more, connect more, rest in God's promises more, worship more, praise more, seek more, soar more, give more and love more. We decree and declare that this is the week of the devil's defeat. We decree and declare that we will operate in the exceedingly abundant overflow of God's grace, in Jesus' name. Amen!

DAY 9

We arise in the power of Almighty God and give orders to our morning and show the dawn its place, take the earth by its edges and shake the wickedness out of it. God, let our prayers meet with You this morning. We command the morning to open her ears to our cry. We command the earth to get in alignment with Your word to receive heavenly instruction on our behalf. We command all the elements of creation to take heed and obey.

Father, we thank You this morning, for this is the day that You have made. We will rejoice and be glad in it. We take the keys of the kingdom today; we bind the strongman this morning and spoil his goods. Father, give us the fruit of our hands and let our own works praise You in the gates. Father, work special miracles with our hands and bring us before great men. We decree and declare that we operate from the place of commanded blessings. We decree and declare that greater is He working in us and through us than he that is in the world (See 1 John 4:4). We thank You for the assurance of Romans 8:28 and praise You in advance that everything is working for our good, in Jesus' name, amen!

DAY 10

Father, we thank You for Your love lifting us from a place of despair, discouragement and devastation. Today we stand on Psalm 30:1-4: we will lift You up, O Lord, for You have lifted us up. You have not let those who hate us stand over us in joy. Lord, our God, we cried to You for help and You healed us. Lord, You have brought us up from the grave. You have kept us alive, so that we will not go down into the deep. Today we sing praises to the Lord because we belong to Him.

We give thanks to His holy name. For his anger is but for a moment but his favor is for a lifetime. Weeping may tarry for the night, but joy comes with the morning.

As for us, we declare, according to Psalm 112:6, "We shall never be moved." We employ the host of heaven to war against the host of darkness and command atmospheric spirits, demonic movements and satanic activities to cease from operating in our lives. We decree and declare that praise is on our lips and will become the meditation of our hearts, because our hallelujahs belong to You!!! We decree and declare a lifting of our finances, fortunes and future. God, lift the heavy load, lift the hands that hang down and problems that weigh us down, in Jesus' name!

DAY 11

Father God, in the name of Jesus, we rise to thank You, praise You and magnify Your holy name. This is the day You have made and we will rejoice and be glad in it. We thank You for Your DIVINE DIRECTIONS and we decree NO MORE DEAD-ENDS! We decree and declare that You are making a way for us in our jobs, in our businesses, in our families, in our churches and in our marriages. Father, we thank You for open doors and divine opportunities.

We speak divine steps, boldness, direction, supernatural intelligence and supernatural wisdom upon our lives, in the name of Jesus! You have brought us out of the fire into a WEALTHY place.

We come against the spirit of depression, sadness, heaviness and lying words that cause us to believe that You are slack or have broken Your promises. But we praise You now for giving us beauty for ashes, the oil of joy for mourning and the garment of praise for the spirit of heaviness!!! We command the spirit of heaviness to be broken over God's people! We break your power, hold and authority satan. We come against the spirit of timidity, fear and failure sent by the devil. We command you to go now in the mighty name of Jesus.

We speak into the womb of this morning and release New Joy and New Strength. We will no longer experience dead-end situations in our jobs, businesses and relationships! We apply the blood and oil of the Lord upon our feet, and declare our feet will no longer run to DEAD WORKS. We thank You for fulfillment and completion of Your plans for us. We command the winds to blow and take our names and place them on the hearts of influential people.

Father, we thank You for connections with Abraham and Boaz, healthy influential connections with billionaires. We thank You that this is the time and season You are causing Your people to invade the marketplace. We will leapfrog over our enemies! We thank You for positioning us in the right place at the right time, in Jesus' name!!!

DAY 12

Father, we thank You that this is the day that You have made and we will rejoice and be glad in it. We decree and declare that no weapon formed against Your people will prosper. We shake out the wickedness that has been set up by the enemy in the four corners of the earth. We decree and declare that doubt, unbelief, fear, distractions and anxiety are removed now, in the name of Jesus. We command the Joy of the Lord to be our strength. We decree and declare that we will no longer operate in frustration or have our peace disrupted. We trust You, Father, and we know that You are working things out for Your people. Every prophecy and promise that You have spoken over our lives is coming to pass for Your people. We decree and declare KINGDOM EXPANSION. We decree and declare GREATER TESTIMONIES and GREATER INCREASE for Your people! We decree and declare New Ideas … New Deals … New Books … Ingenious Inventions and Divine Wisdom. We decree and declare that there is a blessing in the midst of the storm, and we command the Army of the Lord to ARISE! We decree and declare we will walk in stamina, character and integrity, and maximize every door that You open because You have crowned our heads with favor! We decree and declare that we are winning in every area of our lives, in Jesus' name!

DAY 13

Father, this is the day that You have made and we will rejoice and be glad in it. We thank You for Your grace and mercy, and for Your loving kindness towards us today. Father, this morning we rise to dismantle any trap set up by the enemy. We shake out doubt, unbelief, depression and fear that will try to grip us today. We pray for strength for Your people! The spirit of lack and misfortune can no longer dwell in the lives of believers. We thank You for releasing NEW THINGS today!! We thank You now for the open windows, open doors and new opportunities. We receive the downpour of Your abundant blessings. We decree and declare that Your blessings are overtaking us from the north, south, east and west. We are praising You now for making a way through the desert! We thank You for showing and manifesting Your will. We speak TANGIBLE MIRACLES over our lives!

Father, give us the faith to believe You for the impossible. Increase our faith, Lord, and help our unbelief. We decree and declare new plans, new ideas, new inventions, new investments, new property, new positions, new increase, new business, new relationships and new connections! We receive new stamina, fortitude and extraordinary faith! We step into this New Season with great confidence that He who began a good work is able to complete it. Father, we will arise and shine because Your Glory has come.

You give seed to the sower and multiply the seed that has been sown. This is a season of sufficient supply; all of our needs and wants will be met. Father, we are asking that You raise us up as a testimony of Your glory. We expect the impossible everyday and we will finish this year strong. We will finish this quarter walking in grace, authority and power. Our potential will be released.

We speak that this will be a week like no other! We command the womb of this morning to give birth to the will of God concerning our lives. ARMIES OF THE LORD, ARISE! AGENTS OF CHANGE, ARISE! We desire to show forth Your glory, Lord! You said in Your word that we overcame satan by the blood of the lamb, by the word of their testimony and did not love their lives to the death (See Revelation 12:11). We will overcome every distraction sent by the enemy because we are MORE THAN CONQUERORS!! We Expect New Blessings! We decree and declare New Peace, New Joy and New Moves! We have the assurance that it is ALREADY done, in Jesus' name!

DAY 14

Father, we thank You, we praise You, we magnify You and we glorify You. Father, we come this morning with a grateful heart and ask that You take our worship to another level. We thank You for purging us of bitterness, offenses and rebellion. Lord, we come against the hand of the enemy that infiltrates our minds with negative thoughts and memories of dead works. Father, we decree and declare the Shalom of God and we declare good memories for the rest of this year. Lord, we trust in Your name alone. Thank You for restoring our souls and leading us in the path of righteousness for Your namesake. Thank You for loving us!

We decree and declare a deeper love for the things of God and the word of God. We decree and declare that our territories are enlarging and You are getting ready to BLOW OUR MINDS! We decree and declare that all of our prayers are being answered now and You are causing Your favor to surround us like a shield.

We decree and declare that the remainder of this year will be filled with JOY! We speak to the earth this morning and command it to give birth to the fruit of our works.

We decree and declare manifestations, miracles and new memories! Army of the Lord ARISE and TAKE your promises! If God is for us, who can stand against us? God is completing those things which concern us. We decree and declare that all these things are accomplished, in Jesus' mighty name!!

DAY 15

Father, we thank You, praise You, magnify You and give You glory this morning. We thank You for being a Man of Your word. Every word that You have spoken we know is true. We thank You for the light of Your FAVOR shining upon our ways. You are our light and salvation; we will not fear or be afraid.

Father, we thank You that death and life are in the power of our tongue. You said in Your word that if Your people, who are called by Your name, would humble themselves and pray, seek Your face and turn from their wicked ways, then will You hear from heaven, forgive their sin and heal their land (See 2 Chronicles 7:14).

Father, we thank You that divine healing is taking place in our body, mind and soul. We thank You that disease, pain and sickness is leaving our body now, in Jesus' name. We speak to our digestive system, circulatory system, reproductive system and skeletal system and command them to function the way You created them to function. We apply and appropriate the blood upon our bodies now. We command every infirmity in the blood, liver, kidneys, eyes, bones and any cancerous cell to go NOW! You were wounded for our transgressions, bruised for our iniquities, the chastisement of our peace was upon You and by Your stripes we are healed! (See Isaiah 53:5). We rebuke double-mindedness, Alzheimer's disease, forgetfulness, mind games, and schizophrenia! We put on the mind of Christ. We plead the blood of Jesus upon our cranium, cortex, cerebellum and brain stem! Continue to transform us by the renewing of our mind.

Father, now heal the souls that have been broken from past relationships, rejection, rebellion and disobedience. We speak to the spirits of rejection and rebellion and we command them to fall out of agreement with one another. We command the spirits of timidity, fear, perversion, lust, pride, vanity, fornication, adultery, deep hurts, fear of rejection and self-rejection to come up and out in the name of Jesus!!

We destroy the works of every witch, warlock and curse that has been spoken over us, our children, our businesses, our spouses, our homes and our ministries, and return them back to the sender. We thank You for the deliverance, in Jesus' name!! We decree and declare Good News this morning. We thank You for deliverance and breakthrough. We thank You for Your divine healing, wholeness and restoration from the inside out! We release the joy of the Lord upon our lives and our families!!! Restore the JOY of our salvation and remove every thief that comes to steal, kill and destroy our joy! We call it done now, in Jesus' mighty name!

DAY 16

Father, we thank You that this is the day that You have made and we will rejoice in it. We rise this morning to give You glory! We take the earth by its edges and shake out sickness and disease, doubt and unbelief. We declare that all believers are more than conquerors, and we walk in victory.

We come against any backlash, booby-trap and distraction set up by the enemy and we dismantle it now! We put on the full armor of the Lord this morning.

We speak to the earth and command it to yield the harvest that belongs to us.

Lord, let the light of Your favor shine upon our ways. We speak double INCREASE!!!! We thank You for the spirit of CELEBRATION, the spirit of a WARRIOR, and the spirit of a VICTOR. This will be a week of jubilee and testimony! We thank You for stamina to maximize every opportunity. We stand on the promise of Philippians 4:13 NKJV, "*I can do all things through Christ who strengthens me.*" This will be an incredible week!! God, we expect you to do the impossible! We decree and declare that our days are full of possibilities!!! We decree and declare this is the week for DOUBLE miracles, DOUBLE momentum and DOUBLE manifestation. We thank you, Lord, for the increase, in Jesus' name!!

DAY 17

Father, we rise this morning to thank You for Your grace and mercy. We thank You for the unfailing love You've shown towards us. We thank You for the blood of Jesus; for had it not been for the shedding of blood, there would have been no remission of sins (See Hebrews 9:22). We thank You that the last shall be first and the first shall be last. We thank You for calling us out of darkness into this marvelous light. We decree and declare maturity with no further entanglements in every area of our lives. We decree and declare that our anointing is growing, our prophetic anointing is growing, our ability is growing, our grace is growing, and our gifts are growing. We break the yoke of brokenness, bitterness, rebellion and rejection. satan, we bind you and command fear, timidity, low self esteem, abuse and all spirits connected with rejection and rebellion TO GO NOW, in Jesus' mighty name. We command our spirits to grow, flourish and get stronger NOW! We come against foolish talk and immature ways, and choose to walk in Boldness! We will not be scared. We release the power and maturity to grow, now. We decree and declare spiritual maturity and spiritual promotion.

Send increase from the north, south, east and west to our businesses, marriages, ministries, missions, assignments, mandates, mantles, families, sons, daughters, loved ones, churches, pastors and teachers. Lord, give us more stamina for more opportunities! Today is the day of maturity in our Peace, Purpose, Prosperity and Progress, in Jesus' name!! We are closer than we've ever been to our destiny, in Jesus' name!

DAY 18

Father, we thank You because this is the day that You have made and we will rejoice and be glad in it! We take the earth by its edges and shake out lack, poverty, barely enough, doubt, fear and unbelief, in Jesus' name. The blood of Jesus prevails in every area of our lives! We decree and declare that our season of weeping is over and our season of fulfillment is here! We shout with the voice of triumph, "SEND NOW PROSPERITY!!" We release the harvest of influence, harvest of increase and harvest of financial breakthrough. We operate under an open heaven and thank You for holding us up. We decree and declare extreme focus and fortitude, and extraordinary faith upon ourselves. Today we speak OVERFLOW in our mind! Lord we thank You for new thoughts, new ideas, and clever inventions. Lord, let the thoughts in our head become the wealth in our hands. We plead the blood of Jesus over our intellectual property. We decree and declare that we will walk in divine wisdom. We decree and declare that we will walk in a KING'S ANOINTING ... an anointing of influence and increase. We decree and declare that we will penetrate the seven mountains of influence: Arts and Entertainment, Media, Business, Education, the Family, the Government, and the Church. We decree and declare that no weapon that is formed against us will prosper and every tongue that rises we condemn as God's servants. Let the army of God arise and manifest God in the earth! We take authority over every atmospheric spirit. We will maximize every moment, seize every opportunity and grab our prosperity, in Jesus' name!!!

DAY 19

Father, we thank You for Your glory that will be revealed this day. God, we thank You for being mightier than breast cancer, lung cancer, throat cancer, cervical cancer, ovarian cancer and brain cancer. We decree and declare that the nature of God has gone before us this morning. We call on Elohim,

God our Creator, mighty and strong; El Shaddai, God Almighty; Jehovah-Jireh, the Lord will provide; Jehovah-Rapha, the Lord who heals; Jehovah-Nissi, the Lord our banner; Jehovah-Shalom, the Lord Our Peace; Jehovah-Rohi, the Lord our shepherd; Jehovah-Shammah, the Lord is there; and El Elyon, God Most High.

We thank You for green pastures that bring wealth and health to our spirits. We decree and declare that the name, nature and wonders of Jesus go before us. We decree and declare that our angels are going forth to work and fight on our behalf.

We thank You for the name of Jesus that carries power, healing and deliverance. We decree and declare signs, wonders and miracles! We decree and declare restoration, release and restitution. Father, we thank You for Your redemptive work on the cross.

We thank You for covering us with Your love and with Your glory. Lord fill us from the inside out. Today, we decree and declare GRACE UPON GRACE upon ourselves, in Jesus' Name

DAY **20** ———————————————

Father, we thank You, for this is the day that You have made; we will rejoice and be glad in it. Father, we take the earth by its edges and shake the wickedness out of it. Place a hedge of protection of Your blood around believers. We proclaim in the realm of the Spirit that this will be a week of surprises! Let the army of the Lord arise, now. We shall walk in power, strength and authority. Your army is penetrating the seven mountains of influence. Dispatch Your angels and send divine governmental assistance. We thank You for opening doors to major platforms.

We decree and declare that we walk into every opportunity with integrity and character. We declare that this year belongs to us. We are kings and priests unto God; therefore, let the kings arise and walk in influence and decision-making.

Father, we thank You for calling us higher, stretching us and taking us deeper. Father, raise up somebody, somewhere to use his or her influence, power and ability to bless us. We stand on the promise of Amos 9:13 MSG: "*Things are going to happen so fast your head will swim, one thing fast on the heels of the other. You won't be able to keep up. Everything will be happening at once—and everywhere you look, blessings!*

Blessings like wine pouring off the mountains and hills. I'll make everything right again for my people Israel." We thank You in advance for preferential treatment! We expect God to show up and shout for His people, this week, in Jesus' name!

DAY 21 ——————————————⚔

Father, we thank You, for this is the day that You have made; we will rejoice and be glad in it. Father, we take the earth by its edges and shake out the wickedness in every system. We thank You for grace to conquer and OVERTHROW the systems and kingdoms of this world.

We pull down the strongholds of perversion, poverty, prejudice, tradition and religion. We come against the spirits of frustration, fear, anxiety and false burdens.

We command the GRACE OF GOD to be upon every believer. Father, give us grace to MAXIMIZE every moment, idea, connection, finances and open door. Let the light of Your favor shine upon our ways.

We thank You for grace to take our mountains of influence. We step out in faith and walk in victory in the arts and entertainment, government and business, family and church, and media. Father, we thank You for the grace to MANIFEST the will of God on the earth. We speak over our lives new strategies, new ideas and new prosperity in this new season. We are and will be living proof of the glory of God.

We thank You for Your grace and favor, for abundance, overflow, more than enough, and multiplication. We will go back and TRY AGAIN in places of defeat because the Miracle Worker has partnered us. Father, raise up someone, somewhere to use his or her influence, power and ability to bless us. We decree and declare that abundance is our forecast and we will walk in the grace of the God.

Father, we thank You that You are raising up an army and a generation that will be witnesses for You. We thank You that You are raising up a remnant of people who walk in Great Faith. Lord, we yield our vessels to You now for Your Glory. God, send the Rain of Revival, the Rain of Fire, the Rain of the Holy Ghost and the Rain of Breakthrough. We want You to do the impossible here on earth!

Every attack the enemy has set up against the coming revival, we expose it now, in the name of Jesus. We bind every spirit of compromise. Father, cause us to love what You love and hate what You hate. We walk in the breaker anointing. Father, we thank You for authentic praise and authentic worship. We thank You for cleansing, building and launching this great Army of God. Hold us up, Jesus, as we penetrate the mountains of influence in the arts and entertainment, media, church, family education, government and business. We decree and declare that we will be agents of change! Father, take us from Faith to Faith and from Glory to Glory! Father, we thank You for RAISING UP AN ARMY THAT WILL MANIFEST YOUR WILL IN THE EARTH, IN JESUS' NAME!

8 Commanders' Quick Reference Guide
Prayer Terminology and Meanings

THE NAMES OF GOD:

- **El Shaddai:** Lord God Almighty
- **El Elyon:** The Most High God
- **Adonai:** Lord, Master
- **Yahweh:** Lord, Jehovah, The Self Existent One
- **Jehovah Nissi:** The Lord My Banner
- **Jehovah-Raah:** The Lord My Shepherd
- **Jehovah Rapha:** The Lord That Heals
- **Jehovah Shammah:** The Lord Is There
- **Jehovah Tsidkenu:** The Lord Our Righteousness
- **Jehovah Mekoddishkem:** The Lord Who Sanctifies You
- **El Olam:** The Everlasting God
- **Elohim:** The Triune God
- **Jehovah Jireh:** The Lord Will Provide
- **Jehovah Shalom:** The Lord Is Peace

ARMOR OF GOD:
Ephesians 6:14-18

- **Belt of truth:** Protects you from deception
- **Breastplate of righteousness:** Guards your heart with the righteousness of Christ

- **Feet shod with the preparation of the gospel of peace:** feet led by the word and will of God to take you to the hurting and lost

- **Shield of Faith:** Gives total protection against the attacks of satan

- **Helmet of Salvation:** Guards your thought life from the lies of the enemy

- **Sword of the Spirit, which is the Word of God:** Using the word against the enemy as a defensive and offensive weapon:

   Praying at all times in the Spirit, with all prayer and supplication. To that end, keep alert with all perseverance, making supplication for all the saints. **(Ephesians 6:18 ESV)**

AIR TRAFFIC CONTROLLERS:
Intercessors trained to **maintain the safe**, **orderly and expeditious flow of the release from heaven**

to earth. They are sharp shooters in the realm of the spirit who will take out all atmospheric spirits that try to hinder God's plan from manifesting in the earthly realm.

ATMOSPHERIC SPIRITS:
Represent demonic activity in the atmosphere that tries to cause one to deviate from one's destiny. This is an invisible force that tries to hinder visible manifestations of God's power.

BINDING AND LOOSING:
Binding and loosing is a way to take control over atmospheric spirits, satanic activities and territorial spirits.

When the commander binds and looses he draws up a contract in the realm of the spirit and closes the "Gap" between heaven and earth.

DECLARE:
Declaring is speaking into the atmosphere and making known what has already been established by God.

DECREE:
When you decree something you resolve or pronounce a law or course of action predetermined by God.

DISMANTLE:
To strip, separate and take apart piece by piece

ESTABLISH:
To set and fix firmly or unalterably; to settle permanently

GABRIEL:
God's Special Messenger Angel

GATES:
Doorways and entry points into natural or spiritual territories

GROUND CONTROLLERS:
Watchmen who have been commissioned by God to intervene on behalf of others and become **heaven's mouthpiece on earth**

LEGISLATE:
To make something legal, to make it law

MICHAEL:
God's Warring Archangel in charge of regions

REBUKE:
To correct, to reprove and put in place, to condemn

SATANIC GRAVITY:
Demonic power that tries to hold you down and stop you from operating from a place of authority in the third heaven

SYSTEMS OF satan:
- Principalities: Highest ranking demons
- Powers: Witchcraft. Spirits that operate in the power of satan
- Rulers of darkness of this world: Ruling spirits of the cosmos
- Spiritual wickedness in high places: People of influence who are controlled by demonic spirits

NAMES OF satan:
The word "satan" means adversary and enemy of God. He also is known as:
- The Devil: false accuser or slanderer
- Beelzebub: lord of the flies
- Tempter: the wicked one
- Lucifer: light bearer
- Serpent
- Dragon
- Father of lies
- Prince of this world
- god of this age

STRONGHOLD:
Fortified City, Spiritual Fortress in the mind based on satan's lies

WEBSITE REFERENCES:

http://propheticstreams.webs.com/apps/blog/entries/show/7685793-the-eight-prayer-watches

https://www.blueletterBible.org/faq/don_stewart/don_stewart_151.cfm

https://www.merriam-webster.com/thesaurus/carnality

https://sites.google.com/site/soundsintheearth/the-8-prayer-watches

Kimberly Daniels, *Spiritual Housekeeping*, pages 71-72

http://iblp.org/questions/what-significance-using-different-postures-prayer

https://www.challies.com/christian-living/the-posture-of-prayer

http://www.lifeway.com/Article/prayer-postures-in-the-Bible

Thomas Nelson, *Nelson's New illustrator Bible Dictionary*, page 1023

http://Biblehub.com/greek/3794.htm

https://www.gotquestions.org/names-of-satan.html

https://www.blueletterBible.org

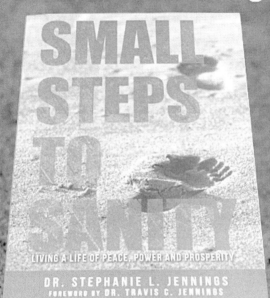

Contact Information

Dr. Stephanie L. Jennings
The Harvest Tabernacle
1450 S. Deshon Road
Lithonia, GA 30078
www.theharvesttabernacle.org
www.prettychics.com